This book of

MAD

verse

is sincerely

dedicated to

YOU,

Dear Reader!

(After such a touching display of
sickening sentimentality, only a
fink would put this book back on
the shelf and not buy it!)

More of William M. Gaines's
MAD Humor from SIGNET

MAD
FOR BETTER OR
VERSE

by Frank Jacobs

Illustrated by
Paul Coker, Jr.

Edited by
Albert B. Feldstein

with a Foreword by
Nick Meglin

A SIGNET BOOK
PUBLISHED BY THE NEW AMERICAN LIBRARY, NEW YORK AND TORONTO
THE NEW ENGLISH LIBRARY LIMITED, LONDON

SIGNET TRADEMARK REG. U.S. PAT. OFF. AND FOREIGN COUNTRIES
REGISTERED TRADEMARK—MARCA REGISTRADA
HECHO EN WINNIPEG, CANADA

SIGNET BOOKS are published *in the United States* by
The New American Library, Inc.,
1301 Avenue of the Americas, New York, New York 10019,
in Canada by The New American Library of Canada Limited,
295 King Street East, Toronto 2, Ontario,
in the United Kingdom by The New English Library Limited,
Barnard's Inn, Holborn, London, E.C. 1, England

FIRST PRINTING, NOVEMBER, 1968

PRINTED IN THE UNITED STATES OF AMERICA

FOREWORD

You're probably wondering why a book of this nature needs a foreword and I'm probably wondering if you're right, but the author probably wondered how he could fill up 192 pages with his ridiculous verse and so asked me to knock it down to 190 by writing a ridiculous foreword. So let's be on with it . . .

Frank Jacobs has been rhyming up the pages of Mad Magazine since he sold us his first poem parodies many years ago. Reader response has always been favorable, most of the mail telling us that "Frank is your verse writer."

nick meglin

nick meglin
Associate Editor
Mad Magazine

I just got a note from Hank Fishman, our typographer, who says the above will not cover the two pages alloted. I have to expand this so that at least one sentence carries over to the next page or Frank will have to write another poem for one of the chapters. Anything but *that!* Out of respect to *you* I'll keep this going as long as I can. Let's see . . . Frank Jacobs . . . oh, yeah! Frank *also* does wonderful song parodies, none of which are included in this book, and none of which, I fervently hope, will ever be included in *any* book, but you never can tell with these money-hungry publishers.

Have I gone over to the second page yet, Hank?

Good.

Okay, dear reader. Turn directly to the first chapter. Do not pass "go," do not collect $200 . . .

CONTENTS

The Village Hippie

Baseball Types

The Night Before Christmas, 1999

Poetry in Everyday Life

The Phone

The Mad Zoo

If Famous Poets Had Different Occupations   1

The Mad Zodiac

If

THE VILLAGE HIPPIE

(with apologies to Henry Wadsworth Longfellow)

Under his pad on 10th and B
The Village Hippie stands;
A turned-on acid-head is he
With pale and shaking hands;
And the flower jacket that he wears
Hangs down in tattered strands!

'ATION

His hair is long and blonde and curled;
He sets it when he can;
His face is caked with unwashed grime
That looks just like a tan;
And when he's near, you sort of wish
He'd use Right Guard or Ban!

13

His pad is just a room for him
To freak out in a crash;
The mouldy mattress on the floor
Contains his secret stash,
In case the Narcs come busting in
To glom his pot and hash!

His roomies, high on boo and coke,
Are fogged in smoky swirls;
And as the Hippie tunes in on
Their dungarees and curls,
He thinks it might be possible
That some of them are girls!

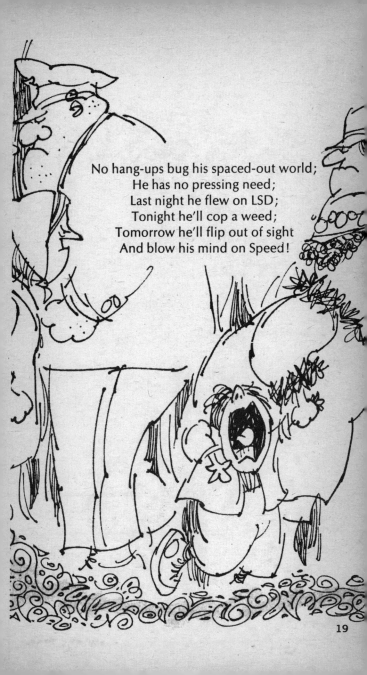

No hang-ups bug his spaced-out world;
He has no pressing need;
Last night he flew on LSD;
Tonight he'll cop a weed;
Tomorrow he'll flip out of sight
And blow his mind on Speed!

The years fly by, and now let's see
The Hippie we once knew;
His hair's turned white; his teeth are gone;
His mind is rotted through;
Who ever thought he'd live to reach
The age of thirty-two!

23

The Pitcher

Before the Pitcher hurls the ball,
He goes into an endless stall:
He wipes his brow, hikes up his pants,
Reties his shoes, adjusts his stance;
It's really not his aim, you know,
To make the game so dull and slow;
It's just without each boring bit
He'd lack the time to work up spit!

The Catcher

Behind ten pounds of pads and mask,
The Catcher has a thankless task;
While pitchers throw and batters swat,
He's in a state of constant squat,
Deflecting fast-balls with his ear
And taking foul-tips on the rear;
Yet, through it all, he'll still persist
Like any normal masochist!

28

The First Baseman

The man at First is just a hulk
Of beefy, burly, brawny bulk;
His only job, the graceless lout,
Is catching balls to put men out;
He isn't fast; he isn't quick;
But no one seems to care a lick;
For, after all, who thinks of style
When he hits balls a country mile!

The Second Baseman

In courage and raw guts supreme,
The Second Baseman leads the team;
As middleman for double plays,
He throws to First, then gulps and prays
That somehow he will save his skin
From spikes and runner crashing in;
Can he avoid this dreadful fate?
Just see him jump—tch, tch—too late!

The Shortstop

We marvel at the Shortstop's art:
Just see him swerve and lunge and dart!
Of course, to some, it makes no sense
Because the ball just cleared the fence;
But in the field the Shortstop knows
That he must put on fancy shows;
How else can he make you and me
Forget he's batting .203?

The Third Baseman

Although he's sprawled out in the dirt,
The man at Third has not been hurt;
He's simply goofed another try
To stab a grounder bounding by;
He's now a mess, to his regret,
Of caked-in dust and grime and sweat;
He's lost the game; now (phew!) let's hope
He hasn't lost his Dial Soap!

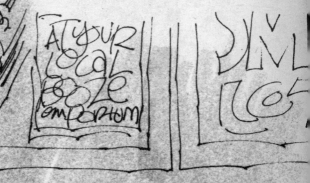

The Outfielders

The man in Center, Left or Right
Presents a most heroic sight;
At crack of bat, he eyes the ball
And races bravely for the wall;
He smacks the concrete with his leap
And crumples in a mangled heap;
Three runs are scoring—what a shame
To lose an exhibition game!

The Manager

The Manager's a mournful gent
With shoulders stooped and body bent;
Although he's not a holy man,
He's learned to pray the best he can;
This afternoon he's forced to see
His club lose 17 to 3;
No wonder that he has one dream—
To manage the opposing team!

THE NIGHT BEFORE CHRISTMAS, 1999
OR
ST. NICHOLAS MEETS
THE POPULATION EXPLOSION

(with apologies to
Clement Clarke Moore)

'Twas the night before Christmas,
    And all through the gloom
Not a creature was stirring;
    There just wasn't room;
The stockings were hanging
    In numbers so great,
We feared that the walls
    Would collapse from the weight!

The children like cattle
    Were packed off to bed;
We took a quick count;
    There were three-hundred head;
Not to mention the grown-ups —
    Those hundreds of dozens
Of uncles and inlaws
    And twice-removed cousins!

When outside the house
    There arose such a din!
I wanted to look
    But the mob held me in;
With pushing and shoving
    And cursing out loud,
In forty-five minutes
    I squeezed through the crowd!

48

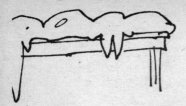

Outside on the lawn
　　I could see a fresh snow
Had covered the people
　　Asleep down below;
And up in the sky
　　What should strangely appear
But an overweight sleigh
　　Pulled by countless reindeer!

They pulled and they tugged
    And they wheezed as they came,
And the red-suited driver
    Called each one by name:
"Now, Dasher! Now, Dancer!
    Now, Prancer and Vixen!
On, Comet! On, Cupid!
    On Donder and Blitzen!"

"Now, Melvin! Now, Marvin!
 Now, Albert and Jasper!
On, Sidney! On, Seymour!
 On Harvey and Casper!
Now, Clifford! Now, Max"—
 But he stopped, far from through;
Our welcoming house-top
 Was coming in view!

Direct to our house-top
    The reindeer then sped
With the sleigh full of toys
    And St. Nick at the head;
And then like an earthquake
    I heard on the roof
The clomping and pounding
    Of each noisy hoof!

Before I could holler
    A warning of doom,
The whole aggregation
    Fell into the room;
And under a mountain
    Of plaster and brick
Mingled inlaws and reindeer
    And me and St. Nick;

He panted and sighed
    Like a man who was weary;
His shoulders were stooped
    And his outlook was dreary:
"I'm way behind schedule,"
    He said with a sigh,
"And I've been on the road
    Since the first of July!"

'Twas then that I noticed
    The great, monstrous sack,
Which he barely could hold
    On his poor, creaking back;
"Confound it!" he moaned,
    "Though my bag's full of toys,
I'm engulfed by the birthrate
    Of new girls and boys!"

Then, filling the stockings,
    He shook his sad face,
"This job is a killer!
    I can't take the pace!
This cluttered old world
    Is beyond my control!
There even are millions
    Up at the North Pole!"

"Now I'm late!" he exclaimed,
    "And I really must hurry!
By now I should be
    Over Joplin, Missouri!"
But he managed to sigh
    As he drove out of sight,
"Happy Christmas to all,
    And to all a goodnight!"

POETRY IN
EVERYDAY LIFE

POETRY
ON THE HIGHWAY

100 feet ahead of you
Is Thruway Exit 22,
Which takes you to the Interstate
By way of Highway 38;
From there on in, take U.S. 4,
Unless your goal is Baltimore;
If that's the case, then take a plane,
Because, you jerk, you're now in Maine!

Poetry in Doctor Bills

Suite 406
Medical Arts Building
401 West 43rd St.
New York City

This bill to you is sent with glee
From Lester J. Monroe, M.D.,
Who last week cured you of the pain
Which you incurred from hangnail strain;
This verse I'm hoping will offset
The case of shock you're sure to get
From learning that you now owe me
One hundred dollars as a fee!

Poetry in Picket Lines

THE GUYS OF LOCAL #4 NOW SEEK

A CONTRACT FOR A 3-DAY WEEK

WITH OVERTIME AT TRIPLE PAY

AND COFFEE-BREAKS 6 TIMES A DAY!

WE HOPE THAT OTHERS UNDERSTA

Poetry in Model Kit Building

This step-by-step instruction sheet
Will make your job an easy feat!

Tangential Spanners C and D
With Bracket Stems N, O, and P . . .

Inserting next the Pivot Pins
To Crossbar 5, which then begins . . .

The flanning of the Lomes, which jut
Above the Central Grommet Strut . . .

Around which Dockles U and V
Are set to spin with Lencers free . . .

Which then afford you room to strip
The edges of each Dockle Tip . . .

And glue Fins 8 and 17
Until the Ormlets riffle clean;

The Phone

(with apologies
to Edgar Allan Poe)

See the salesman on the phone—
Public phone!
Calling Minnesota on a deal he can't postpone!
Ah, what anger he is feeling
As he tries to make his call!
Hear him bellowing and squealing
'Cause he's reached a bar in Wheeling
When he thought he had St. Paul!
Hear him shout, shout, shout
That his quarters have run out—
That he's lost the operator and can't get a dial tone!
On the phone, phone, phone, phone,
Phone, phone, phone—
On the money-eating, outdoor, public phone!

See the housewife on the phone —
Kitchen phone!
Gabbing with a neighbor in a boring monotone!
Her poor husband's tried to reach her
That he's fired from his job,
That their daughter's socked her teacher,
And their son's a filthy creature
Who has joined up with the mob!
See him call, call, call,
But he has no luck at all!
For the line's tied up forever with the housewife's
Endless drone!
On the phone, phone, phone, phone,
Phone, phone, phone —
With the gabbing of the housewife on the phone!

See the bookie on the phone —
Private phone!
Taking bets on horses in his sleazy undertone!
See the fortune he has made off
All the suckers now in hock!
For the cops have all been paid off
And the Chief has called the raid off
That was set for three o'clock!
Making book, book, book,
Till the suckers all get took!
Making thousands from their wagers till their
Savings they have blown!
On the phone, phone, phone, phone,
Phone, phone, phone —
On the bookie's own unlisted private phone!

See the doctor on the phone —
Office phone!
Talking to a woman who is speaking in a moan!
She is feverish and aching
And she's lying on the floor!
But the doctor's head is shaking
As he tells her he's not making
Any house-calls anymore!
Hear her beg, beg, beg
That she's got a broken leg!
But the doctor kindly tells her that she's only
Bruised a bone!
On the phone, phone, phone, phone,
Phone, phone, phone!
On the doctor's ever-handy, office phone!

See the broker on the phone —
Wall Street phone!
Talking to investors in a confidential tone!
See how artfully he's told them
They should buy his gold-mine stock!
See the way that he's cajoled them
And the cunning way he's sold them
Each a whopping giant block!
How they'll swear, swear, swear
When they find the mine is bare —
And the broker's current whereabouts are
Suddenly unknown!
On the phone, phone, phone, phone,
Phone, phone, phone —
When they find he's got a disconnected phone!

See the snooper on the phone —
Someone's phone!
Monitoring phone-calls in his office all alone!
He can tap most any wire
That is linked to any spot!
And he always finds a buyer
Who is eager to acquire
What his dirty work has got!
How he'll grin, grin, grin
When he rakes the money in —
From the private talk of others that's no business
Of his own!
On the phone, phone, phone, phone,
Phone, phone, phone!
On some helpless victim's not-so-private phone!

THE MAD ZOO

The Camel

The camel is, to say the least,
A most unsightly, smelly beast;
You'd think, to see his pair of humps,
He'd caught a case of backward mumps;
He never makes attempts to hide
His sullen, stubborn, stupid pride;
That's why I'm sure I'll never see
A camel walk a mile for me!

The Python

The python loves to crush his foes,
   Which ultimately dooms them;
And when they're in their final throes
   He quietly consumes them;
Right now he's feeling quite depressed
   And hopes someone will guide him
To find a method to digest
   The tourist that's inside him!

The Yak

The yak sits like a mammoth mop,
    A shaggy apparition;
He won't go near a barber shop
    And runs from the beautician;
He bellows with a dreadful roar
    But, still, he won't attack us;
He's much too busy looking for
    A young, seductive yakess!

The Eel

The eel's a power-plant of volts
That shoots electrifying jolts
  Right through his frame, so slippery and greasy;
But though he's all charged up to kill,
The eel will not feel right until
  He finds out if he's AC or he's DC!

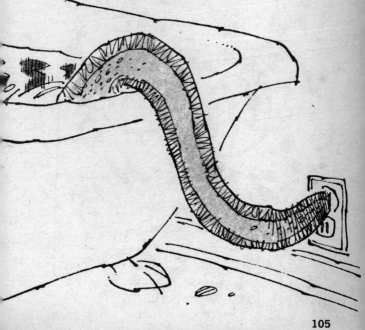

The Tiger

The tiger is, we must assume,
　　A very hungry feline;
He is, therefore, a beast for whom
　　We shouldn't make a beeline;
But should you wander near his pad,
　　Remember this, my precious,
Unlike that Coca Cola ad,
　　His paws do not refresh us!

The Aardvark

For snobbery and sheer conceit
The snooty aardvark can't be beat;
   His self-esteem is absolutely tedious;
What makes the Aardvark act this way?
Because he just found out today
   He's listed first in our encyclopedias!

The Ostrich

Observe the silly ostriches
  Stick their heads in sand there;
The stupid birds think lost riches
  Lie beneath the land there!
But don't forget how strong they are,
  Obstinate and sullen;
For if you say how wrong they are
  They will kick your skull in!

The Opossum

The possum's found
Above the ground
In forest, wood and dale;
A branch or limb
Is home to him
And thereby hangs a tail.

The Bat

Bats are creepy; bats are scary;
Bats do not seem sanitary;
Bats in dismal caves keep cozy;
Bats remind us of Lugosi;
Bats have webby wings that fold up;
Bats from ceilings hang down rolled up;
Bats when flying undismayed are;
Bats are careful; bats use radar;
Bats at nighttime at their best are;
Bats by Batman unimpressed are!

The Skunk

Whenever there's
A skunk with airs,
We always seem to smell him;
The fault's not his;
The problem is
His best friend will not tell him!

118

The Zebra

The zebra says, with great delight,
His stripes are black, his coat is white;
Tomorrow he will take it back
And say his stripes are white on black;
Small wonder that we've come to doubt
The double-talk he's handing out;
In truth, he really is, of course,
A psychedelic mini-horse!

The Crocodile

We know that cats like liver
And that roosters holler "Cockle-doo"!
But in a jungle river,
No one's sure just what a croc'll do!

It's said he's fond of creeping
To the places where small fishes nap,
And, as they lie there sleeping,
To consume them with a vicious snap!

He has no favorite dishes
For he makes no special plan for lunch,
And if he can't find fishes
He may even have a man for lunch!

So if, by chance, you wind up
In his jungle river, then you, sir,
May find that you've been lined up
For the crocodile's menu, sir!

The Shrew

Unawed by gnus
Or caribous
Or elephants or camels,
The shrews are proud
To be endowed
As nature's smallest mammals;

Should shrews refuse
To stay in zoos,
It's wrong to hold them blameable
For if you've read
What Shakespeare said,
You'll know they're rarely tameable!

The Dolphin

Behold the ocean's gadabout—
   The frisky, friendly dolphin;
His head displays a smiling snout;
   His backside sports a tall fin;
Content to frolic in the sea,
   He's never mean or warlike;
How happier our world would be
   If dolphins we were more like!

IF FAMOUS POETS HAD HAD DIFFERENT OCCUPATIONS

If
RUDYARD KIPLING
were a
Cookbook Editor

You can talk of beef and spuds,
When you're frocked in fancy duds,
A'sittin' there as cozy as you please;
But when some heathen demon
In your stomach starts a'screamin',
Then you'll sell your bloomin' soul for Buttered Peas.

For it's Peas, Peas, Peas!
They're enough to bring a blighter to his knees!
I'll give up those flying fishes
Long as I've big, heaping dishes
Of those succulent, delicious
Buttered Peas!

First you shell 'em to the man,
Then you dump 'em in a pan,
And boil 'em till the bugler calls a halt;
Next remove 'em neat and clean,
While you shout, "God Save the Queen!"
And then serve 'em with some butter and some salt!

For it's Peas, Peas, Peas!
There's no finer food in all the seven seas!
It's for you I give my pay for,
Walk the road to Mandalay for;
To the God above I pray for
Buttered Peas!

If
WALT WHITMAN
were a
Greeting Card Writer

O Valentine! My Valentine!
Your face is everywhere;
I see it in the dead leaves;
I see it in the toadstools in the wood;
I see it in the lake scum and the swamp moss;
But I do not see it in the peat bogs;
O Valentine!
You are the bullfrog croaking and the jackal
    howling and the buzzard screaming,
And occasionally the gopher thinking;
My heart is nature's toothpaste tube, and
    you are the force eternal that squeezes
    out the final, itsy-bitsy sweetness;
O me!
O you!
O me! O you!
O you! O me!
O us!
O Valentine!

If
ROBERT W. SERVICE
wrote the
Weather Report

A mass of cool air is churning it up
    Down the whole Atlantic coast,
And out in the West it's so dog-dirty hot
    That it's making a rattlesnake roast;
In Ohio some snow is beginning to blow
    And they're due for a blizzard or two;
And up in the skies, folks are peeling their eyes
    For the Hurricane known as Sue!

In north Idaho nights are 50 below
    From a cold front up Canada way;
And that low-pressure mass that had started to pass
    Just keeps hanging around day to day;
They're choking from dust from a high-pressure gust
    That keeps blowing from Texas right through;
And from here to Moline folks are looking real keen
    For that Hurricane known as Sue!

138

They're flooded from rains on the Great Western Plains,
    And from Michigan on to the East,
They're starting to freeze from a cold, icy breeze
    That ain't fit for a man or a beast;
You all wonder, I guess, from this weatherman's mess,
    If the forecast's for rain or for shine —
If everything fails, flip a coin heads or tails,
    'Cause your guess is no better than mine!

If
CARL SANDBURG
were a
Baseball Writer Covering
The New York Mets

Play Butcher of the League,
Goof Maker, Dropper of Flies,
Booter of Grounders and the Nation's Ball-Fumbler;
Hitless, runless, winless,
Team of the Big Blunders:
They tell me you are losers, and I believe them; for
    I have seen your hitters be thrown out trying to
    stretch a bunt into a triple.
And they tell me you are deficient, and I answer: Yes,
    it is true I have seen your clean-up man go 0-for-5,
    get benched, then return to go 0-for-5 again.
And they tell me you are hopeless, and my reply is:
    On the faces of your rookies I have seen the marks
    of grief and despair.
And having answered I ask myself: How is it possible
    that nearly two million fans buy tickets every year
    to see the Play Butcher of the League, Goof Maker,
    Dropper of Flies, Booter of Grounders, and
    Ball-Fumbler to the Nation?

If
EUGENE FIELD
Sold
Fresh Fish

Herring, Salmon, and Cod are out,
  So better take something else—
Why not Flounder or Rainbow Trout?
  Or maybe a dozen Smelts?
Mackerel's tasty and, if you wish,
  My Haddock I'll guarantee;
I'll sell you almost any fish
  That comes from the beautiful sea;
  But kindly don't be asking me
          For Herring,
          Salmon,
          Or Cod!

I've Whitefish and Bluefish, Swordfish and Pike;
    My Fluke is a steal for the price;
Red Snapper's delicious, or maybe you'd like
    A Bass that's especially nice;
Sturgeon is making an elegant dish;
    My mullets are fine as can be;
I'll part with almost any fish
    That comes from the beautiful sea;
    But kindly don't be asking me
            For Herring,
            Salmon,
            Or Cod!

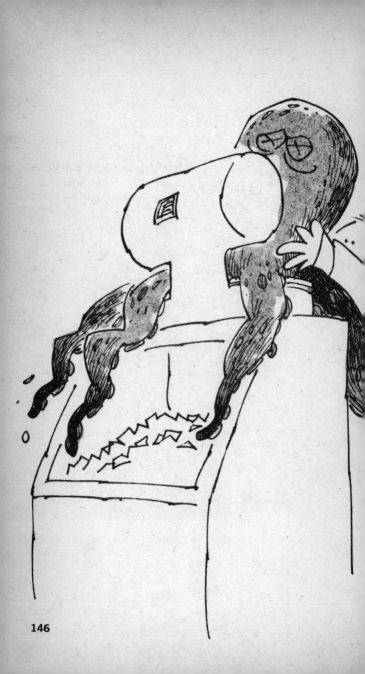

I've Catfish and Dogfish, Minnows and Eels;
   Perchance you are craving some Squid?
A Marlin will give you a dozen good meals—
   I'll throw in a pot and a lid;
As soon as you're telling me what you wish
   I'll wrap it in paper for free;
I'll let you have most any fish
   That comes from the beautiful sea;
   But kindly don't be asking me
      For Herring,
      Salmon,
      Or Cod!

If
WILLIAM BLAKE
were a
TV Critic

Huntley! Huntley, on my screen,
Dullest newsman I have seen!
What infernal network plan
Makes thee such a boring man?

Brinkley! Brinkley, cute and bright,
Coining quips each weekday night!
How doth NBC permit
Thy superficial, silly wit?

Huntley! Brinkley! Deadly pair!
Giving newscasts I can't bear!
Why do I sit in distress
When Cronkite's there on CBS?

If
LEWIS CARROLL
were a
Hollywood Press Agent
In the Thirties

'Twas Bogart and the Franchot Tones
    Did Greer and Garson in the Wayne;
All Muni were the Lewis Stones,
    And Rooneyed with John Payne!

"Beware the deadly Rathbone, son!
    Don't Dumbrille with the Carradine!
Beware that you the Greenstreet shun!
    And also Bobby Breen!

He took his Oakie firm in hand:
    Long time the Bracken foe to seek —
He stopped to pray at Turhan Bey,
    And murmured, "Donald Meek."

And like a Lorre Brent with hoods,
    The deadly Rathbone, eyes Astaire,
Came Rafting through the Donald Woods,
    And Karloffed everywhere!

Sabu! Sabu! And Richard Loo!
     The Oakie gave a Hardwicke smack!
He seized its Flynn, and with a Quinn,
     He went Fontaining back!

"And didst thou Duff the Rathbone, Ladd?
     Come Grable in the Eddy, boy!
O Alice Faye! O Joel McCrea!"
     He Cagneyed in his Loy.

'Twas Bogart and the Franchot Tones
     Did Greer and Garson in the Wayne;
All Muni were the Lewis Stones,
     And Rooneyed with John Payne!

THE MAD ZODIAC

Aries the Ram

(Mar. 21 – Apr. 19)

Kazowee! Smash! Bang! Biff and Bam!
No wonder Aries is the Ram!
The only way his ego thrives
Is butting in our private lives;
We bolt our doors, but we can't win —
The Aries pounds till he gets in;
And once he's entered, have no doubt,
An atom bomb can't get him out!

Taurus the Bull

(Apr. 20 – May 20)

When there's a party you can't stand,
You'll find a Taurus right on hand
Offending crowds of helpless folks
With ancient, dull and endless jokes;
To make things worse for one and all,
The punch-lines he cannot recall;
Few things upon this earth can bore us
Like the bull of some old Taurus!

Gemini the Twins

(May 21 – June 21)

A Gemini is kind and mean,
Refined and rotten, foul and clean;
In other words, we must confess,
He's just a schizophrenic mess;
But though he's filled with peace and strife,
He tries to live a normal life;
He'll make a faithful friend and mate —
Well, half of him, at any rate!

Cancer the Crab

(June 22 – July 22)

It takes most people quite a spell
To know a crab-like Cancer well;
And when they do, we must confide,
They're often sorry that they tried;
But though his outlook's gray and grim,
It pays to be a friend to him;
If so, you'll see his spirits zoom
From deep depression up to gloom!

Leo the Lion

(July 23–Aug. 22)

A Leo comes on with a roar,
And when he's through, he roars some more;
He does this so we'll plainly see
That in his world there's one boss — he!
He's glad to share your point of view
As long as it is his view, too;
But should you cross him, have no fear —
The welts will fade within a year!

Virgo the Virgin

(Aug. 23 – Sept. 22)

A Virgo will not hesitate
To tell you that you're second-rate;
For exercise he strains his wits
At finding faults and picking nits;
At night he murmurs soft and clear,
"I love you so, my precious dear;"
We know his sentiments are true,
For it's himself he's talking to!

Libra the Scales

(Sept. 23 – Oct. 22)

From just a brief, initial look,
A Libra seems a hopeless schnook;
At second glance, we soon detect
Our first impression was correct;
His house is filled with friends who mooch,
Who borrow cash, who drink his hooch;
Let's hope his giving never ends;
We'd hate to see him without friends!

Scorpio the Scorpion

(Oct. 23 – Nov. 21)

If you should see a Scorpio,
Then, goodness gracious, say hello!
For if his presence you ignore
He'll soon declare a private war;
However, if you're over-nice,
You'll pay an even bigger price;
For once he says your friend he'll be,
You'll never need an enemy!

Sagittarius the Archer

(Nov. 22 – Dec. 21)

A Sagittarius, you'll find,
Will say whatever's on his mind;
From what he says, we must conclude
What's on his mind is pretty crude;
He's right at home in drunken brawls,
In street-gang fights and free-for-alls;
He wishes he could get a job,
But who can use a one-man mob?

Capricorn the Goat

(Dec. 22 – Jan. 19)

A Capricorn's a hapless goat
Who always seems to miss the boat;
The shirts he washes end up shrunk;
He buys a car; it turns to junk;
His life's a roll of endless craps
That even fouls up other chaps;
Because of his unlucky sign,
I couldn't make this last line rhyme!

Aquarius the Water-Bearer

(Jan. 20 – Feb. 18)

There's little reason to discuss
The fuzzy-brained Aquarius;
His mind is in the stratosphere;
The rest of him is barely here;
Psychiatrists throw up their hands
And mutter things about his glands;
In truth his problem is clear-cut:
He's just a happy, harmless nut!

Pisces the Fish

(Feb. 19 – Mar. 20)

The ardent Pisces loves to feel
He's one great mass of sex appeal;
You'd think by now that he would see
The girls who date him don't agree;
But though he falls flat on his face,
He simply can't give up the chase;
No wonder life's a string of crises
For the luckless, love-sick Pisces!

IF

(with apologies to
Rudyard Kipling)

If you can change a tire on the thruway,
  While stranded in the busy center lane;

If you can find a foolproof, tried-and-true way
  To housebreak an impossible Great Dane;

If you can find another way to open
   A sardine tin when you have lost the key;

If you can find a fumbled bar of soap in
 Your shower when the suds won't let you see;

If you can buck a mob of lady shoppers
    And get outside without a scratch or bite;

If you can get a dentist for your choppers
    To fix a toothache on a Sunday night;

If you can smack a truck with your jalopy
    And make the driver think he was to blame;

If you can be a loafer, poor and sloppy,
  Yet have the world think you're some famous name;

If you can rid your house of dull relations
   By faking mumps or plague or Asian flu;

If you can go through tax investigations
And somehow wind up with them owing you;

If you can read these verses as we list 'em
    And answer "Yes" to each and every one;
Then, Charlie, you have really licked the system —
    And now we wish you'd tell us how it's done!